National Park Sites

MOLOKAI

Kalaupapa National Historical Park

MAUI

LANAI

Haleakala National Park

KAHOOLAWE

HAWAII

**Puukohola Heiau
National Historic Site**

**Puuhonua o Honaunau
National Historical Park**

**Hawaii Volcanoes
National Park**

*Mauna Kea, at 13,796 ft.,
is the highest peak in the Hawaiian Islands.
It is a dormant volcano.*

HAWAIIAN NATIONAL PARKS

In Cooperation with the National Park Service

A SUNRISE BOOK

CONTENTS

A waterfall at Oheo Gulch, Kipahulu,
part of Haleakala National Park, coastal unit.

Published by Sunrise Publishing, a Sequoia Company,
Santa Barbara, California

Edited by Nicky Leach

Design and Illustrations by Linda Trujillo

Maps by Frank Becker

Typesetting by Graphic Traffic

Printed in Japan
ISBN: 0-917859-11-1

ACKNOWLEDGEMENTS

This book could not have been produced without the assistance of those who dedicate
their lives to the greater appreciation of Hawaii's natural and historic resources. We
would particularly like to thank the following: Gary Beito at the USS *Arizona* Memorial
and Kathy English at the Hawaii Natural History Association for their constant support
at all stages of this important project; Bryan Harry of the National Park Service, who
contributed to this book and reviewed its contents; the Bishop Museum, Hawaii State
Archives, US Geological Survey, National Park Service, National Geographic Magazine
and Camera Hawaii for their help with photography. Finally, we are grateful for the
contributions of the fine authors and photographers who have enriched this publication.

PHOTO CREDITS

Ellis Armstrong: 11 (middle right); **Frank S. Balthis:** Cover (bottom middle), 24 (top right);
Bishop Museum: 30; **Camera Hawaii:** 43 (top right); **Maxine Cass:** 43 (bottom), 44 (top), 45
(bottom); **Ed Cooper:** Cover (background, middle, bottom left), back flap (bottom), title spread,
6, 10 (top), 11 (bottom upper right), 16, 22, 24 (top left), 28, 32 (bottom), 34, 40, 48; **Betsy
Harrison-Gagne:** 19; **William Gagne:** 20 (top); **Hawaii State Archives:** 37 (middle), 43 (top
left); **Hawaii Volcanoes National Park:** Front flap (top), back flap (middle), 13 (bottom) by Bob
Siebert, 15 (middle), 25 (top), inside back cover (top); **Kim Heacox:** Back flap (top), 11 (bottom
right); **Paul Henning:** Cover (top right), 45 (top); **Hugo Huntzinger:** Back cover, 18 (top); **Maile
Kjargaard:** 18 (inset); **Henry G. Law:** Cover (bottom right), 37 (top), 38, 39 (bottom); **Anwei
V. Skinsnes Law:** 39 (top); **Ronald J. Nagata:** 20 (bottom left); **National Park Service:** Cover
(top left) by Kepa Maly, front flap (bottom) by Gil Tanaka, 24 (bottom), 26, 27, 31, 32 (top), 33
(top), 35, 37 (bottom); **Pat O'Hara:** 21; **Steve Raymer:** 33 (bottom) © 1983 National Geographic
magazine; **Roger Robinson:** 14; **Charles Seaborn:** 20 (middle right); **Allan Seiden:** 40; **USS
Arizona Memorial:** 42, 44 (bottom) by Jerry L. Livingston, 44 (inset bottom); **US Geological
Survey** by J.D. Griggs: 8, 10 (bottom), 12 (top & bottom left), 13 (top), 15, inside back cover
(bottom); by Toni Duggan, USGS: 12 (bottom right); by R.I. Tilling, USGS: 11 (bottom left);
Ed Wood: 46

Introduction

Bryan Harry

Pacific Area Director
National Park Service

Painting of the iiwi bird
by Bryan Harry.

M ost people who visit national parks in mainland North America take their diversity for granted—from Everglades to snowclad Rocky Mountains, Civil War battlefields to Mesa Verde cliff dwellings. But few are aware of the equal diversity and enormous range of national parks in our nation's Pacific islands.

Isolated across an ocean far more vast than North America, these islands are a different place with strikingly distinctive biota, history, archeology and geology from mainland or continental places. The best examples of these phenomena lie within the national parks.

Some are alive geologically—volcano islands forming even now, often in continuous eruptions. People have witnessed these eruptions for hundreds of years as chronicled in numerous Hawaiian myths and oral histories. Terms such as Pele's hair, Pele's tears, Pelean eruptions, and pahoehoe and aa lava types, have crept into scientific terminology of volcanism.

It should come as no surprise that Pacific parks and historic sites are often a mixture of cultural, natural, scientific and scenic places unlike any other place on Earth. They range widely in themes—Pearl Harbor and the Pacific island battlefields as the Park Service's only World War II sites and interpretation; the greatest

and most active volcanoes on earth; deserts stretching across the lee side of large volcanoes; pristine, tropical rain forests with endemic birdlife that would have awed Charles Darwin on the wet windward mountainsides; Hawaiian cultural and archeological temples; and an isolated settlement for those suffering from Hansen's Disease (or leprosy), where Father Damien was instrumental in changing our perception of people afflicted by this dreaded disease.

The people who have authored the following pieces on the island parks are steeped in knowledge of these places. They have lived here and personally observed their subjects. Mostly, they are caretakers of these superb public places and regard their jobs as a kind of public trust. They are the best interpreters of each of the parks for you. Though small, the parklands are complex and they can tax your endurance and understanding. But they are well worth the effort.

Most people who visit one or more of the island parklands ultimately return again and again. We know this as most of the contributors to this book have become so entrapped. So, if you wish not to be addicted to the Pacific islands, stop here. These great examples of Pacific islands' natural and historical wonders are subtly contagious.

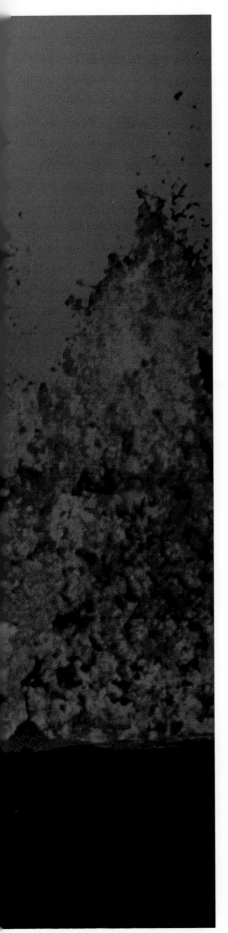

HAWAII

Hawaii Volcanoes National Park

T he eruption of one of Hawaii's famous volcanoes is not just a spectacle, it is a total experience. The combination of the shaking ground, the jet-like roar of the fire fountains, the sulphurous smell and radiant heat from the molten lava, and the stunning sight of a fountain of fire playing high in the air and falling into a lake of glowing lava stays in one's memory forever.

But these vivid displays of Nature's awesome power are considered "quiet" in contrast to volcanoes in other parts of the world where, because of different lava composition, eruptions are devastatingly explosive. The nature of Hawaiian eruptions makes this one of the best places in the world to witness Nature's greatest show.

Hawaii Volcanoes National Park makes it possible for the traveler to see all this beauty, mystery and dynamic geology at close range. The park was established in 1916 to protect, interpret and make accessible the bizarre volcanic landscape of Kilauea Volcano, as well as the rain forests, rare plants and birds that exist there. The original park included the summit caldera and north flank of Mauna Loa Volcano as well as Haleakala Volcano on Maui. It was later expanded to take in the Kalapana section of the coast, and Haleakala became a national park in its own right.

Preserving Hawaiian Wildlife

The task of preserving Hawaii's unique wildlife from destruction is an important one. In no place in the world have so many diverse species evolved from so few ancestors. But, with the encroachment of the diseases and practices of civilization, many of the islands' native flora and fauna have now disappeared. Introduced domestic animals such as pigs and goats have gone wild and destroyed many delicate habitats, a problem which is being eased by an ongoing fencing program.

The variety of species continues to astonish scientists; new plants, birds and insects are being discovered even today. Visitors to Hawaii Volcanoes can witness the range of this diversity themselves: the famous nene or Hawaiian goose, acacia koa trees, tree lobelias, and several varieties of hibiscus.

The famous "curtain of fire" fountains along the Kilauea East Rift during a 1983 eruption.

9

Halemaumau Crater in Kilauea Caldera.

Wahaula Heiau

Just within the park boundary, at the Kalapana coastal entrance, stands the **Wahaula Heiau,** the 13th-century site of the temple of the Red-mouthed God, one of the oldest heiau (temples) in Hawaii. This high-walled temple was believed to have been built according to the edict of Paao, high priest of the conquering chiefs. Wahaula changed the worshipping rituals of Hawaii's people by the introduction of human sacrifice to appease the red-mouthed war god, Kukailimoku. A small museum here displays exhibits about the lives of the ancient Hawaiians. A nature trail also leads from the archeological ruins past unique plants, coastal vistas, and ancient areas of human habitation.

Viewing The Park

Chain of Craters Road, periodically closed when one of Kilauea's frequent eruptions buries it under lava flows, connects the summit of Kilauea with the coast. It was first opened in 1965, but just four years later a long-lasting eruption began, and extensive lava flows eventually covered more than 12 miles of the new road to as much as 300 feet deep. After reconstruction, the road was reopened in 1979. It crosses glistening black lava flows that look as if they've hardly cooled, and affords dramatic views of the huge flows that poured down Kilauea's slopes into the ocean between 1969 and 1974, adding 150 acres of new land to the Big Island.

Mauna Loa and Kilauea are two of the most active—and certainly the best-studied—volcanoes in the world. Since 1912, the Hawaiian Volcano Observatory, perched on the edge of Kilauea Caldera, has monitored the heartbeats and blood pressure of these volcanoes for a twofold purpose: to increase the general knowledge of volcanic activity, and to try to lessen the hazards for those living in the shadow of volcanoes by more accurate forecasting of eruptions.

Hawaiian Volcano Observatory

The observatory was founded by Dr. Thomas Jaggar, who at that time was Professor of Geology at the Massachusetts Institute of Technology, but later devoted

U.S. Geological Survey scientists leveling near Puu Oo on Kilauea's East Rift.

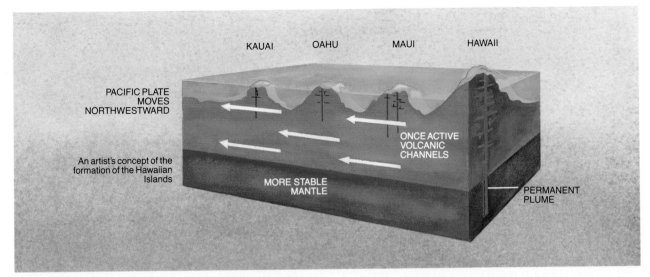

KAUAI   OAHU   MAUI   HAWAII

PACIFIC PLATE
MOVES
NORTHWESTWARD

ONCE ACTIVE
VOLCANIC
CHANNELS

An artist's concept of the
formation of the Hawaiian
Islands

MORE STABLE
MANTLE

PERMANENT
PLUME

his life to studying Hawaii's volcanoes. At first a private endeavor supported by MIT and the Hawaiian business community, the Hawaiian Volcano Observatory was, for a time, administered by the National Park Service, but has been part of the U.S. Geological Survey since 1947.

Observatory scientists use sophisticated instruments to monitor changes in volcanic activity. A large network of seismographs locate the size and intensity of the hundreds of earthquakes—mostly unfelt—that jiggle the Big Island daily. Instruments called tiltmeters measure the uplift of the mountains; a volcano gently swells as it inflates with molten lava prior to an eruption. These and other scientific studies are bringing the dream of eruption forecasting closer to reality.

In 1987, the Hawaiian Volcano Observatory will move to a new research laboratory now being built near its present site, and the current building will become the Jaggar Museum. Exhibits will explain the interior structure and dynamics of a model Hawaiian volcano,

and will also tell the geological story of the origin of the Hawaiian Islands.

Hawaii's Fiery Beginnings

Geologists have determined that the age of the islands follows an unusual progression. The lava rocks of Kauai are five or six million years old, Oahu's are two to three million, Maui's are about one million, while those of the Big Island are all less than one million years old.

Scientists now believe that the Earth's surface is broken into about 10 plates which are slowly moving in relation to one another. Most volcanoes are found at the edges, where the plates pull away or override one another. Occasionally, though, there is a "hot spot" beneath the middle of the plate, generating a series of volcanoes as the plate moves slowly over it. Hawaii, in the middle of the Pacific plate, seems to be over one of these hot spots which send a plume of molten rock to the surface. Since the plate is moving over it at a rate of about four inches a year, the conduit through which

SUMMIT CALDERA

CENTRAL VENT

MAGMA RESERVOIR

How a shield volcano works.

Aa lava.

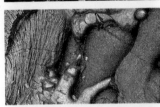

Pahoehoe lava.

Pele's hair.

Lava river near a prehistoric cinder cone on Mauna Loa's Northeast Rift during March 1984 eruption.

the lava flows eventually gets bent over too far; a new conduit then forms, and another volcano starts building.

The last time a Hawaiian island emerged from the sea was about a million years ago, when Kohala volcano broke the ocean's surface with the first rocks of the Big Island. Today, this island is composed of five volcanic centers: Kohala, Mauna Kea, Hualalai, Mauna Loa and Kilauea, all in different stages of life.

Kohala, deeply eroded, is presumed to be dead. Mauna Kea has not erupted in 3,600 years but probably still could; Hualalai's last eruption was in 1801—just yesterday in geologic time. After a 25-year rest, Mauna Loa had a brief eruption in 1975, and then burst to life again in 1984 with a spectacular three-week eruption that sent a lava flow almost to the outskirts of Hilo.

Arching fountain during February 1983 eruption along Kilauea's East Rift.

Scientists measure lava temperature during March 1984 eruption on Mauna Loa.

A forest of lava trees at the Kilauea East Rift.

Recent Eruptions

Kilauea has been very active recently. In January 1983, an eruption began on Kilauea's East Rift Zone (about 10 miles from the summit caldera) that has continued—in episodes lasting a few hours to a few days—until this writing. A rift zone is a region of weakness in a volcano's sides along which underground cracks occur; when lava moving underground is injected into these cracks, an eruption can break out many miles from the summit. There have been more than 45 eruptive episodes so far, separated by periods of repose that last, on average, about a month. These eruptions are characterized by high lava fountaining. Cinders and spatter have built a cinder cone more than 800 feet high which has been given the name Puu Oo (Hill of the Oo, an extinct bird that used to nest in that area).

In early 1984, one of the Puu Oo eruptions occurred while Mauna Loa was also in eruption—the first time in 65 years that two Hawaiian volcanoes have erupted simultaneously. Besides affording a spectacular visual display, that event provided scientists with another piece in the puzzle of understanding the volcanoes' underground structure. It has long been assumed that Mauna Loa and Kilauea are both fed by the same deep Hawaiian hot spot, but some observers have thought that there was also a much shallower connection and that the activity of one would affect the other. That proved not to be the case; Puu Oo erupted on the same schedule it had kept before the Mauna Loa eruption started, and did not seem to diminish (or increase) Mauna Loa's activity in any way.

Another recent discovery is that—as the hot-spot theory would predict—a new volcano seems to be silently growing under the sea about 30 miles southeast of the Big Island. Scientists have detected evidence of undersea eruptions taking place there, and analysis of rocks dredged from the top of the new seamount—which has been named Loihi—confirms that they are very young. If Loihi's growth follows the traditional pattern, in about 10,000 years the Hawaiian chain should have a new island, and Pele will have a new home.

Mauna Loa's Northeast Rift during the March 25-April 15, 1984 eruption.

Lava flow burns a forest during the simultaneous eruption at Kilauea, March 30, 1984.

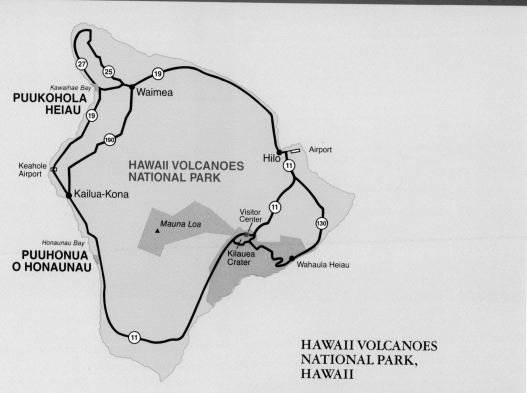

HAWAII VOLCANOES
NATIONAL PARK,
HAWAII

Location

Hawaii Volcanoes National Park is located in the south-eastern section of the Big Island of Hawaii, about 96 miles from Kona and 30 miles from Hilo.

Information

Driving distances within the park are not especially long—the principal roads total about 45 miles—so it is possible to see the highlights of the park in just one day. Much better, though, is a stay of two days (or more), which allows time to take some of the short hikes that so enrich the understanding and enjoyment of the park.

In either case, the best starting point for a tour is at **Park Headquarters and Visitor Center,** where there is a small but up-to-date museum with exhibits about the main features of the park. A volcano film that is shown hourly is a good introduction to volcanic eruptions, and especially helpful in getting oriented is a large relief model of the Island of Hawaii on the Visitor Center porch.

Check at the Visitor Center for maps, back country permits (for overnight hikes), information, and a wide range of publications with more detailed information about the park's geology, natural history and history.

Driving

The **Crater Rim Drive** (exit left out of the Visitor Center) makes an 11-mile circuit of Kilauea Caldera, winding first through a lovely lush rainforest of native ohia trees and tree ferns. Be sure to stop at all the overlooks for fine views and interpretive exhibits along the way. After about four miles, the road descends into the south end of Kilauea Caldera on the edge of the **Kau Desert**—a desert caused mostly by acid rain from volcanic fumes.

Cycling Chain of Craters Road.

The road passes **Halemaumau firepit,** the focal point for Kilauea's volcanic activity, and legendary home of Pele. It then starts the climb back out of the Caldera, crosses the deep cracks of the Southwest Rift Zone, and passes the **Hawaiian Volcano Observatory.** After passing a side road that leads to **Bird Park** and the Mauna Loa strip, you will come to an area of steam vents and sulphur banks on your left. Close by, **Volcano Art Center,** housed in the historic 1877 Volcano House, features an art gallery and art and craft workshops. The circuit is completed at the Visitor Center.

The **Chain of Craters Road** starts from the Crater Rim Drive about 3½ miles from the Visitor Center, and follows Kilauea's East Rift Zone. The craters along this road show where eruptions have occurred in the distant—and not so distant—past.

After the Mauna Ulu road turnoff, the Chain of Craters road leaves the East Rift and zigzags down the south flank of the mountain to the sea and to **Wahaula Heiau.**

Volcano House: caldera side.

Devastation Trail.

Hiking

Be sure to save time to take several of these short hikes along the way—some are less than a mile long, but all are scenic and enjoyable: **Earthquake Trail**—starts across from the Visitor Center, 0.6 miles round trip, striking evidence of damage from the November 1983 earthquake; **Thurston Lava Tube**—starts from Crater Rim Drive, 0.5 mile loop through a jungle-filled crater and a 400-foot lava tube; **Devastation Trail**—starts at Puu Puai overlook off Crater Rim Drive, 1.2 miles round trip, boardwalk trail through area devastated by the 1959 Kilauea Iki eruption; **Bird Park (Kipuka Puaulu)**—starts from Mauna Loa Strip Road, 1-mile loop trail through lush native plants in an island of vegetation surrounded by young lava flows; **Puuloa Petroglyph Trail**, starts from Chain of Craters Road, 2 miles round trip, to a field of rock pictures carved by early Hawaiians; **Ke Ala Kahiko Trail**, starts from Wahaula Heiau Visitor Center, 1-mile trail along sea cliffs and ancient Hawaiian ruins.

Some of the longer hikes in this area are very rewarding.

One of these, Kilauea Iki Trail—starts at park headquarters and ends at Thurston Lava Tube. The 5-mile trail descends into the site of the 1959 lava flow. For information on any of the fine longer hikes, inquire at the Visitor Center.

Food and Accommodation

The only hotel accommodations inside the park are at **Volcano House**, (reservations necessary). Meals are also available there, with reservations required for dinner. Additionally, snacks may be purchased in Volcano House. Meals are available just outside the park in Volcano Village and at the Volcano Golf and Country Club. Gas is available in Volcano Village.

There are three campgrounds in the park—one near Kilauea, one on the Hilina Pali Road, and one along the Kalapana coast. Cabins with the use of showers are operated at one of the campgrounds, Namakani Paio, by the Volcano House. Primitive cabins are also available in the Mauna Loa backcountry and the coastal section of the park. These can only be reached by trail and registration at park headquarters is required.

Volcano Art Center.

MAUI

Haleakala National Park

Rising cool and clear above the clouds, Haleakala is located in a setting of stunning natural beauty and subtle nuances, ranging from a moonlike landscape of colorful cinder cones and lava flows, to dense jungle and wild ocean headlands.

Maui, one of the younger islands in the Hawaiian chain, began as two separate volcanoes on the ocean floor. After emerging from the sea, lava, ash, and alluvium eventually joined the two by a valley, forming Maui. Water erosion then took over and cut deep depressions into the summit area of Haleakala. Two of these depressions finally met and created the "crater" we see today.

Further volcanic activity partially filled the crater with lava and cinder cones, so that today it resembles a true volcanic crater. Haleakala has not erupted for several hundred years now, although there is a possibility of future activity. As the volcano moves northwest away from the plume that feeds it, it is destined to become extinct.

The original park area was set aside in 1916 to protect the unique and unforgettable volcanic panorama of the large summit crater. Kipahulu Valley and the adjacent rain forest were added to the park in 1969 to preserve their virgin and fragile native ecosystem which contains many rare and endangered plants and animals. In recent years, the Kipahulu coastline also has been included. Haleakala National Park, along with Hawaii Volcanoes National Park, was declared an International Biosphere Reserve by UNESCO in 1980.

The First Settlers

Today's visitors to the Islands arrive within a few hours by jumbo jet, but it wasn't so long ago that the very first visitors reached these shores by outrigger canoe. These early arrivals from distant Polynesian islands called the volcano Haleakala—the House of the Sun—because they said the demi-god Maui had snared the sun here to slow its passage across the heavens. Scattered throughout the park (as well as the summit crater) are important cultural and religious sites.

In much the same way, the ancestors of Hawaii's native plants and animals also made this great journey, one so fraught with danger that, on average,

The dramatic sweep of Haleakala's summit crater.

17

The Kipahulu rain forest. Inset: The rare parrotbill, found only in the Kipahulu rain forest.

only a single new species survived every 10,000 years. Isolated from continental influences by over 2,000 miles of hostile, open ocean, the younger islands of the Hawaiian archipelago offered a great variety of virgin habitats. This environmental diversity, from tropical to alpine, desert to rain forest, encouraged the few successful early plant and animal colonizers to explode into hundreds of new species.

The result is that no place of comparable size equals Hawaii in its variety of new plant and animal species; more than 95 percent of the islands' flowering plants and 99 percent of the insect species are found nowhere else. These evolutionary phenomena overshadow even Darwin's famed Galapagos Island discoveries. Hawaii represents a world-class natural laboratory of evolution, genetic diversity, and adaptation to survival within a great variety of living conditions.

For millions of years, Hawaii's flora and fauna were fortunate never to have to coexist with terrestrial mammals and predatory ants and snails. Plants whose ancestors possessed thorns, nettles, tough bark, or poisonous alkaloids in order to survive were allowed by virtue of their unique environment to evolve in literally thousands of directions.

A Conflict Between Man and Nature

Yet, as rich and beautiful as these islands are, they have also suffered unprecedented losses of native species. Over half of Hawaii's birds, mollusks, and lowland insects, and 10 percent of her flowering plants, have been lost as a direct and indirect result of Man's interaction with this island environment.

Entire species and subspecies are often restricted to single islands, isolated ridges, and other specialized, easily-disrupted environments. For this reason, they have been very susceptible to habitat disturbances, especially those resulting from the deliberate or accidental introduction by settlers of domesticated animals, predators, aggressive alien plants and diseases. Freed from harsh winters and predators, and presented with relatively defenseless vegetation, many of these introduced species went wild.

No comparable area in the world has lost so much genetic diversity. More than one-third of the extinct species of the entire United States are Hawaiian, as are at least one-third of the world's endangered birds and plants. By far the greatest losses have occurred since the arrival of western man. However, recent discoveries in a cave in the southwestern rift zone of Haleakala show that extinction of Hawaii's bird life and native forests probably began with the arrival of the first Polynesians about 1,600 years ago. Bones of more than two dozen new bird species were found—nearly half of them flightless.

The continuing introduction of aggressive plants and animals has rapidly increased the rate of destruction so that within the next century Hawaii may well lose many, if not most, of her remaining native birds, plants and invertebrates unless effective action is taken soon.

Discovering Haleakala's Treasures

Many examples of nature's will to survive against all odds endure, hidden from view. At Haleakala National Park, these include such fascinating creatures as carnivorous caterpillars, flightless moths, fish that climb 200-foot-high waterfalls, giant "picture wing" fruit flies, and colorful native birds with strange beaks that

One of the rare lobelias to be found in the rain forest.

were once sought by ancient Hawaiian royalty.

Between the crater and nearby rain forest, high-elevation bogs support miniature ohia rain forests—mature trees only a few inches tall—that are restricted to econiches of only ½ acre. And buried in the soil beneath them are thousands of years of the earth's climatic history, as well as part of Maui's biological evolution, locked up in a multitude of pollen layers. Close by, amid the jungle mists, are several rare lobelias, some with floral sprays three feet across, which are rapidly being destroyed by the wild pigs that roam the park.

Along the south side of the crater, Maui's dry forests, considered to be the richest in plant species of all Hawaiian forest types, once stretched around the lower flanks of Haleakala. Now largely destroyed by cattle and wild goats, only a few isolated pockets of native trees and shrubs tenuously survive. Two of Hawaii's three known lakes are found on the opposite or wet side of the crater, providing perhaps the rarest of all environments within the entire state. And hidden in

Dr. Robert Robichaux from U.C. Berkeley takes leaf samples for water balance experiments from a greensword in a bog.

The pinao, the largest dragonfly in the world, makes its home in Haleakala.

nearby fog-shrouded bogs, giant greenswords (cousin of the famous silversword) shoot up seven-foot-high spikes.

In a remote corner of Maui, to the east of Haleakala Crater, is Kipahulu, one of the Islands' most dangerous and remote valleys. Its dense and little-explored rain forest receives nearly 400 inches of rain per year, and probably contains many species of plants and invertebrates yet to be discovered.

Saving the Resources

Haleakala ranks high among national parks due to the complexity of its resource management problems. Protecting the numerous small ecosystems from the ravages of destructive wild animals is a full-time job.

Though now largely controlled at Hawaii Volcanoes National Park, wild goats and large European pigs, gifts from Captain Cook and Captain Vancouver nearly 200 years ago, have turned large areas of Hawaii's forests into weedy, rock pastures and muddy wallows. As plant cover is destroyed, the steep mountain slopes are quickly eroded down to bedrock. Not only are critical community watersheds and the quality of drinking water threatened, but some scientists now believe that silt reaching the ocean is killing Hawaii's offshore reefs and associated fish life.

Since 1951, over 12,000 feral goats have been removed from Haleakala Crater (including 2,400 in 1984). Yet a 1985 survey indicated that approximately 2,000 still remained. At Hawaii Volcanoes National

A bog in the Upper Hana Forest Reserve. Right: The same bog three years later after devastation by wild pigs.

Park, which is much larger, it was not uncommon to round up several thousand during a weekend drive. A massive fencing program begun there 15 years ago has proved extremely successful; today, no feral goats are known to remain within the fenced portion of that park.

Fencing the Park

Until 1975, it was an accepted fact that fencing would not work in Haleakala; the terrain and logistics were thought so formidable that goats and pigs could never be controlled. However, with the continued dedication and efforts by park staff, help of volunteers, and emergency funding, fencing has been shown to be viable in the park. The National Park Service now provides major funding for fence construction. By the end of 1986, the impossible will have been accomplished—Haleakala Crater will be enclosed by a 32-mile fence which will control those animals within the park and will keep out the goat and pig hordes in the future.

Although a second major fencing effort is now underway in the remote rain forests of Kipahulu Valley, dealing with resource management problems at Haleakala goes far beyond goats and pigs. For example, alien predators (mongooses, rats, cats and dogs) threaten the long-term survival of all Hawaiian birds and invertebrates. And two continental insects now threaten many native insects, some of which are essential to pollinate the beautiful silverswords and other native plants. In addition, there are at least 150 species of alien plants within Haleakala. Emphasis will soon be shifting to preventing the spread of strawberry guava, pine,

Fencing the park.

blackberry, gorse, eucalyptus, and other alien "weeds."

The Nene and the Silversword

Possibly the two most famous Hawaiian examples of successful conservation are the Hawaiian goose (nene) and the Haleakala silversword (a-hina-hina). Only a half-century ago, these two beautiful symbols of "Aloha" numbered less than 60 wild birds within the State and perhaps less than a hundred plants along the western rim of Haleakala Crater—a drastic change from the 1873 report which described the summit area as being "covered by thousands of silverswords..."

Fortunately, both of these native species have been saved from extinction. Today, there are approximately 100 wild nene at Haleakala and several hundred in and around Hawaii Volcanoes. And within Haleakala Crater, more than 45,000 silverswords now march across the colorful cinder cones.

Rescued from extinction: the beautiful silversword and (inset) the Hawaiian goose or nene.

Planning the Future

Interested readers are encouraged to become involved in protecting the environment. One way to help save the resources in our national parks is by direct participation in a volunteer service trip. This often involves wilderness camping and working directly with park rangers on specific projects. A second and equally important way to participate is to donate money and supplies in support of specific park projects.

Haleakala National Park demonstrates the positive effect man can have on his environment when the desire for conservation is strong. A visit to the park is an experience to savor—a chance to come face to face with one of the most unique environments on earth.

HOW TO VISIT

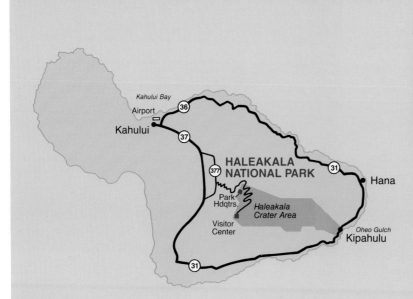

Hiking inside the crater at Haleakala.

HALEAKALA NATIONAL PARK, MAUI

Location

Haleakala National Park, located on East Maui, extends from the 10,023-foot summit to the sea coast of Kipahulu. Though not directly connected by road, these two sections of the park are accessible by car from Kahului airport.

How To Get There

Haleakala Crater, located 11 miles past the park entrance, is a 40-mile (1½ hour) drive via highways 37, 377 and 378 from Kahului. The **Oheo** (Kipahulu coastal) section of the park is at the southeast end of Maui. It can be reached via a 62-mile drive from Kahului around the north (wet) side of the island on scenic highway 36. Allow at least three hours one way.

Information

Park Headquarters is located one mile inside the park entrance. Here Park Service personnel furnish general information, permits, and publications. Exhibits in the center address some of the daily problems facing the park.

The **Visitor Center** is located 10 miles ahead and 2,800 feet higher at the edge of the crater. Besides a magnificent view of the crater, exhibits here explain the geology, archeology, and ecology of the park, as well as the wilderness protection programs. During the day, a park ranger is on duty to answer specific questions and to give interpretive talks.

Overlooks with orientation panels and exhibits are located at **Leleiwi, Kalahaku** and **Puu Ulaula** on the road to the summit. The rare silversword can be seen at Kalahaku, and if cloud conditions are right, the "Specter of the Brocken" can be seen at Leleiwi. A small information station is operated at Oheo by the Hawaii Natural History Association.

Hiking

Haleakala National Park is a true wilderness. It can best be appreciated by spending time hiking in the back country. There are approximately 32 miles of hiking trails in the park. Three main trails take the visitor into the Crater: Halemauu Trail, Sliding Sands Trail and Kaupo Trail.

Further information about camping and hiking in the park is contained in a brochure available from Park Headquarters.

Food and Accommodation

There are no food services, stores, service stations, or overnight motel accommodations within the park. You should plan on bringing your own food into the park, and make sure you have plenty of gas in your car for the round trip. Primitive campgrounds are available by car at Hosmer Grove (Park Headquarters) and at Oheo. Two other campgrounds, accessible only by trail, are located within the crater wilderness. Primitive cabins are also available within the crater, by reservation only. Inquire at Park Headquarters.

Tips

Weather near the summit is unpredictable and varies considerably. Winters tend to be cold, foggy and windy, with a rare snowfall. Summers are milder, but may quickly turn wet and cold. Weather conditions for viewing the crater change from hour to hour. You are advised to dress warmly when visiting the crater. The Kipahulu coast is subtropical and showers can occur at any time.

The chance to witness a sunset or sunrise at Haleakala should not be missed.

21

The Hale o Keawe at Puuhonua o Honaunau.
It was reconstructed in 1985.

Puuhonua o Honaunau National Historical Park

Discovery of the Hawaiian Islands by the early Polynesians was probably accidental. Reasons for their voyages were varied — famine, chiefs looking for new places to establish dominion, young chiefs expelled by established chiefs, or escaping from wars. They used the sun, ocean swells and currents, and the moon and stars as a compass until seabirds and clouds indicated that land was close at hand.

Historians believe that the first wave of Polynesian voyagers probably came from the Marquesas Islands to the south, about 1,500 years ago. Then, about 700 years ago, the early settlers' lives were disrupted by the arrival of a more aggressive and vigorous people (from the Society Islands, it is believed, also to the south) whose culture overwhelmed that of the earlier people.

No one knows when the area of Honaunau was first settled by these intrepid people. They had sailed close to 3,000 miles of unknown seas in their 60-foot double canoes lashed together with strong cord. This was a feat rivaling even those of the Phoenicians, celebrated for their sailing prowess in European history.

The Polynesian double canoes carried dried fruit and vegetables, pigs, dogs and jungle fowls for meat. They also brought taro, sugar cane, coconut, bananas and breadfruit plants, in case they chanced upon a barren island on which to settle. No children came, and in many cases, goodbyes were forever. It is believed that one woman for every three men made the journey for purposes of procreation, as space was limited. It seemed that colonization would be difficult, and yet, some say that 300,000 Hawaiians inhabited the islands at the time of Captain Cook's arrival in 1778.

The lives of the early Hawaiians were strictly controlled by religious beliefs. There were four major gods in their religion — Kane, Kanaloa, Lono and Ku — as well as myriad lesser gods and goddesses, including Pele, the volcano goddess. The gods were considered all-powerful, closely followed by the paramount chief, the high chiefs and the high priests. At the bottom of the line were the commoners and a class comparable to the Indian Untouchables.

The Hawaiians believed in *mana* or spiritual power. The paramount chief was thought to possess the greatest mana among mortals. In fact, his power

23

Kii or effigies of Hawaiian gods guard the Puuhonua at the ocean entrance.

The great wall at the Puuhonua o Honaunau.

was such that commoners were required to prostrate themselves whenever a conch shell announced his approach. Any commoner who did not do so, or who allowed his shadow to fall on the chief's residence might be executed.

Kapu

Kapu was a system of do's and don'ts that governed the everyday lives of the Hawaiians. For example, *do* prostrate when a sacred chief approaches, *do not* look at him, commoners *do* serve the chiefs, women *do not* eat pork and bananas, men and women *do not* eat together, and other such restrictions.

The penalty for breaking a kapu was severe. It usually meant death unless a kapu-breaker was able to reach the safety of a puuhonua (place of refuge) and be absolved by the priest. Such a place was the Puuhonua o Honaunau.

The Place of Refuge

There is no indication when the area on the south shore of Honaunau Bay was designated a puuhonua. History tells us that the great stone wall that encloses the place of refuge was probably built about the year 1550. The wall is dry-laid, without mortar, and held together by friction. It measures about 10 feet high, 17 feet wide, and 1,000 feet long. Built in an L-shape, the northern leg measures over 600 feet in length, the other leg about 400 feet, with the sea forming the third leg of the triangle. The whole area encompasses about 12 acres.

At the seaward end of the north wall was the *Hale o Keawe* (House of Keawe), a temple built about 1650 to house the bones of Keawe-i-kekahi-alii-o-ka-moku. His mana, and that of 22 other chiefs whose bones were subsequently deposited within the temple, gave sanctity to the puuhonua.

Everyone, including rival chiefs, firmly believed that to violate the sanctity of any place of refuge would displease the gods and incur their wrath. They and their followers would then surely be destroyed by a volcanic eruption, lava flow, hurricane or tidal wave. The puuhonua system worked because everyone believed in it.

The Puuhonua o Honaunau was used by chiefs and commoners alike. There was a resident priest within the walls. The sanctuary was used not only by those who had violated a kapu, but also by noncombatants and defeated warriors escaping wars, women and children, and the sick and maimed.

Those who came to the puuhonua from the north had to swim into it because the Palace Ground adjoined the north wall. The king and queen resided there, using 10 or more different thatched houses. Each served a separate function: eating, sleeping, praying, and working.

Those seeking sanctuary from the south could enter the place of refuge by land. This was the entrance used by women and children, the sick and the maimed.

The royal procession is part of the 3-day cultural festival at the park.

All puuhonua were considered sacrosanct. (The idea arrived with the early immigrants from the Society Islands.) However, only in Hawaii could a violator emerge from a place of refuge and return home to resume a normal life as though nothing had happened. The system worked because there was a strong belief that no one would dare to leave a puuhonua before being absolved of their crime for fear of displeasing the gods.

There were also other types of puuhonua in Hawaii. A king was himself able to be a puuhonua. A kapu-breaker could rush to a king to ask forgiveness, although that was risky since the king could also order his death. Queen Kaahumanu, Kamehameha's favorite wife, was a puuhonua.

Life Inside the Refuge

Once inside the puuhonua, the refuge seekers were safe from their pursuers, normally the king's warriors. Those in pursuit were not permitted within the sacred grounds. Any who dared to enter were immediately slain by the priest as they had broken a kapu.

The absolution ceremony performed by the priest could take either a few hours or a couple of days, depending on the nature of the violation. Defeated warriors and army deserters entered the refuge and remained there until the war ended. Even women and children, and the old, sick and maimed were unsafe outside these walls during battle.

Food and water were not a problem in the puuhonua as the tidepools and ocean were rich with sea life. Drinking water, though brackish, was available; the Hawaiians were used to drinking it. Shelter was also not a problem as Hawaiian skin was used to the island sun and ample trees offered shelter. Nights could be spent outdoors due to the warm climate. However, the sanctuary did not offer the comforts of home and most left as soon as they could.

Building the Refuge

The story of the Puuhonua o Honaunau traditionally begins with the building of the Great Wall enclosing it, around 1550. At that time, the temple lay close to the middle of the stone enclosure. Today, it is called the Old Heiau since its original name is lost. It is also said that another was built next to it, named the Alealea Heiau.

In 1650, the Ka Iki Alealea (The Little Alealea), now known as the Hale o Keawe, was built at the ocean end of the north wall of the Great Wall, where it still stands. The Hale o Keawe was reconstructed in 1968, and again in 1985.

Folklore tells us that the Alealea Heiau replaced the Old Heiau. Some time after the Hale o Keawe was built, the Alealea became the chief's family temple.

Kamehameha

The Honaunau area was ruled continuously by King Kamehameha's family even before the Great Wall was

The hukilau or net fishing is a popular part of the cultural festival.

Kaipo Moses demonstrates canoe carving at the park.

Reconstructing the Hale o Keawe in 1985.

built. The region began to receive more attention in Hawaiian history following the death of King Kalaniopuu, Kamehameha's uncle, in 1782. Kalaniopuu's body was brought from the south district of Kau to a spot adjacent to the Place of Refuge of Honaunau. A large shed was constructed in which the king was laid. His bones were later deposited in the Hale o Keawe to add more mana to the place of refuge.

Over the next nine years, a bloody war ensued between Kamehameha and Keoua Kuahuula and Kamehameha's cousin, Kiwalao, Kalaniopuu's son and heir. Kamehameha took possession of Kiwalao's lands in 1782, those of Keoua in 1791, and subsequently those of other Island chiefs by 1810, thereby unifying the Hawaiian Islands.

In 1812, Kamehameha returned from Honolulu to Kailua on the island of Hawaii. From there, he ran the affairs of his kingdom and turned his attention to agriculture. On May 8, 1819, Kamehameha died and his son, Liholiho, assumed the throne as Kamehameha II.

The Influence of the West

Kamehameha II's father, posthumously known as Kamehameha the Great, had continued to embrace the old religion, despite the fact that he witnessed kapu broken daily by foreigners. Doubtless he realized that his power over the people depended on maintaining the restrictions of the old religion.

However, urged by his mother, Keopuolani, and his stepmother, Kaahumanu, Kamehameha II bowed to the inevitable, and sat with the women to eat in November 1819. This broke the basic rule of all kapu that forbade men and women from eating together. The king then ordered all the temples destroyed. Only the Hale o Keawe at Honaunau and the Hale o Lono at Waipio Valley were spared.

The Hale o Keawe was never taken apart, even though Queen Kaahumanu had the bones in the temple removed and ordered it dismantled in 1829. During the 1840s, it was reported that the temple still stood, albeit in ruins. The Great Wall, too, was no longer maintained.

In the next hundred years following the abolition of Hawaiian religion, the Honaunau area declined as people moved away to higher elevations where the days were cooler, and jobs became more plentiful as western concepts began to take hold.

No surface structures remain in the Palace Ground, save the Royal Canoe Landing and the Royal Fishponds, as the area has been inundated by tsunami (tidal waves) and high winter surfs many times since 1819.

In 1920, Honaunau became a county park and carried the name of City of Refuge. This was a misnomer that began in 1823 when missionary William Ellis likened the puuhonua to the biblical cities of refuge. In November 1978, the U.S. Congress restored its rightful name at the request of the Association of Hawaiian Civic Clubs, as Puuhonua o Honaunau National Historical Park.

The park today is expanding its interpretation, cultural festivals, reconstruction and restoration programs, and new structures. The completion of a new highway to the park has expanded visitation to over 350,000 visitors a year. Many visitors say that the mana still pervades the region. People return time and again because the park gives them a good feeling.

A hula demonstration during the cultural festival.

HOW TO VISIT

The "Avenue of Flowers" leads to the park.

PUUHONAU O HONAUNAU NATIONAL HISTORICAL PARK, HAWAII

Location

The park is located about 30 miles south of Keahole Airport and 22 miles south of Kailua-Kona. It is 76 miles from Hawaii Volcanoes National Park.

Getting There

Visitors coming from Kailua-Kona or Keahole airport should turn right onto Highway 160 after passing the 104-mile marker on Highway 11. Those coming from Hawaii Volcanoes National Park should turn left onto Highway 160 after passing the 103-mile marker. Highway 160 to Puuhonua o Honaunau National Historical Park is a 3.5-mile drive along the "Avenue of Flowers."

Information

The first point of contact is the Visitor Center information desk where you should pick up a brochure containing self-guiding information to the park. Three audio messages along the story wall next to the information counter tell about the Polynesian migration to Hawaii, the concept of refuge, and the place of refuge. Twenty-minute orientation talks in the amphitheater are presented daily at 10:00, 10:30, 11:00 a.m., and 2:30, 3:00 and 3:30 p.m.

Special Events

Special programs are presented at the park throughout the year. These range from daily demonstrations of native arts and crafts to monthly talks by guest speakers on Hawaiian history, culture, crafts, and archeology. Hula demonstrations and semi-annual sports days featuring ancient Hawaiian games are also popular.

The biggest event of the year is the annual three-day cultural festival, held on the weekend nearest to the beginning of July, the park's establishment-day anniversary. Each day features a different theme. Numerous cultural activities such

as lei making, featherwork, tapa making and nose flute making offer a fascinating opportunity to learn a Hawaiian handicraft. Additional features of the festival are the royal court processions, the hukilau (Hawaiian community net-fishing technique) and food tasting.

Weather

The weather on this part of the Big Island of Hawaii is subtropical. Cool clothing and sunscreen are recommended. In case of showers come prepared with a light raincoat.

Tips

No matter what time of year you visit, the park encourages you to allow yourself time to learn about a craft. There is always at least one cultural demonstrator carving a kii (image), pounding tapa (bark cloth), doing featherwork, or weaving a coconut frond bowl. Call ahead to see what demonstration is being performed that day.

Groups numbering less than 25 who wish to study Hawaiiana or environmental education at the park may stay at the dormitory for a small fee. Program arrangements may be made with Kahua Naau Ao at the park.

27

Moonrise over Puukohola Heiau

HAWAII

Puukohola Heiau National Historic Site

Today, only the stone platform of the great heiau (temple) built by Kamehameha the Great remains. Though only the shell of the temple, the stacked stone structure is still an impressive sight when viewed from the ocean below.

The story begins in the year 1782 when Kamehameha's uncle, King Kalaniopuu, died. For service, skill and bravery on the battlefields, Kalaniopuu had, before his death, appointed Kamehameha the guardian of Kukailimoku (Ku, the land grabber), his family war god. Kiwalao, his older son, had been designated as heir apparent. To his younger son, Keoua Kuahuula, he gave the districts of Kau and Puna, and to his half-brother, Chief Keawe Mauhili, the districts of Hilo and Hamakua, to administer for Kiwalao.

After Kalaniopuu's death, his body was brought from the district of Kau to the village of Honaunau in Kona for the funeral services. Kamehameha conducted the ceremony.

However, there was already animosity between the competent Kamehameha and Kiwalao. When Kamehameha handed the sacred *awa* drink he had prepared during the ceremony to his cousin, Kiwalao simply passed it on to one of his chiefs. This was a grave insult to Kamehameha. The stage for conflict was set.

In the ensuing Battle of Mokuohai, fought on land and sea, between Honaunau Bay and Kealakekua Bay, Kamehameha defeated and killed Kiwalao. Thus, Kamehameha became the ruler of the Kona and Kohala districts.

But Kamehameha dreamed of conquest. The star with the tail (Halley's Comet) had foretold his greatness at birth. As a young man, he had also moved the Naha Stone. It was said that he who moves the stone will rule Hawaii. Today, that stone lies on the grounds of the Hilo library, daring anyone else to move it.

Construction of Puukohola Heiau

Kamehameha battled unsuccessfully with Keoua Kuahuula for several years before seeking advice from a renowned seer named Kapoukahi who lived on Kauai. The prophet said that Kamehameha must build a great temple to his

Kamehameha the Great.

A wooden effigy of Kukailimoku.

war god on Puukohola (Hill of the Whale) in Kawaihae.

It was a difficult task, for Kawaihae is a desert. Construction began in the hot summer of 1790 with the appropriate religious ceremony. The heiau needed to be a *luakini,* a temple of the highest order, and everything was to be blessed with a religious ceremony as each stage of the temple was completed. The presiding priest had to be of the highest rank; Keliimaikai, Kamehameha's brother, was chosen.

Hundreds of people were recruited to assist in the construction and to pass the red waterworn stones from hand to hand in a human chain from as far away as Pololu Valley, a distance of about 14 miles. These stones were then dry-laid, without mortar.

Even Kamehameha helped in this gigantic effort. His brother Keliimaikai also felt compelled to help when he noticed this and picked up a stone. Kamehameha immediately scolded his brother and had the stone taken out in a canoe, beyond the horizon, and dumped into the sea. It was absolutely necessary that the priest remain pure.

Word soon reached the other chiefs on the island that Kamehameha was building a great heiau to the war god at Puukohola. They also knew of the prophesy of Kapoukahi, that they would be conquered by Kamehameha if he were to complete the heiau.

The kings of Maui, Molokai and Oahu had also heard of the prophecy and knew that Kamehameha would be unbeatable if he completed the heiau. To prevent this, they launched a combined invasion toward Kawaihae.

Kamehameha Receives Help from the West

Kamehameha received word that an invasion was on its way, and met the invaders with his armada of canoes, some mounted with cannons, off the coast of Waipio Valley. In the ensuing Battle of the Red-Mouthed Gun, he routed the enemy, using the talents of ex-sailors John Young and Isaac Davis.

Davis had been captured in 1789 off Kaupulehu in North Kona when the Hawaiians attacked and captured a ship, *Fair American,* in retaliation for the flogging and throwing overboard of one of their chiefs by Captain Metcalf of the *Eleanora* a few days before. The captured ship happened to be captained by Metcalf's son, unbeknownst to the Hawaiians. Isaac Davis alone of the crew was spared because the Hawaiians were impressed by his bravery and ferocity in battle.

Meanwhile, Captain Metcalf was anchored in Kealakekua Bay waiting for his son's ship to join him. While he was there, a messenger brought news to Kamehameha on shore of the capture of the *Fair American.* Fearing retaliation, Kamehameha placed a kapu on the bay so that no Hawaiian would go to the ship and accidently let Metcalf know what had happened.

John Young, a crew member of Metcalf's, happened to be on shore at the time and found that he could not get back to the ship because of the kapu. After a period of time, Metcalf tired of waiting for his son, sailed away, and left Young.

Kamehameha soon gained the loyalties of Davis and Young, and they played prominent roles in future wars. Davis died in Honolulu in 1810. Young was made governor of the island of Hawaii in 1802 by Kamehameha, a position he held until 1814 when he asked to be relieved. Kamehameha then made him a Hawaiian chief, which was until that time an inherited position. Young married Kamehameha's niece and his granddaughter Emma subsequently became queen. When Young died in 1835, he was entombed in the Royal Mausoleum in Honolulu with other Hawaiian royalty.

Pele Helps the Cause

While Puukohola Heiau was being constructed, Kamehameha launched a small invasion toward Maui and Molokai. He was forced to make a speedy return when his cousin, Keoua Kuahuula, began to invade his territory by going around the east side of the island. His uncle, Keawe Mauhili, was killed en route for sending warriors to help Kamehameha.

This painting by Herb Kane suggests what constructing the heiau might have been like.

Kamehameha repulsed his cousin and Keoua started back for the district of Kau via Hilo. A part of his army went south by way of Kilauea Volcano. Soon after they passed by Halemaumau Crater, there was a tremendous steam blast from the volcano that hurled ash and stones, and blanketed the area for miles with choking, poisonous gas. Footsteps in the hardened volcanic ash remain today in Hawaii Volcanoes National Park, witness to the fact that the warriors ran in every direction in a vain attempt to escape the gas.

The way was now clear for Kamehameha to complete the heiau. There were no more interruptions and the work went quickly. The impressive heiau was finally completed in the summer of 1791. A heiau of that magnitude demanded a human sacrifice of the highest order. The logical one was Keoua Kuahuula.

Kamehameha sent two of his counselors to Kau to invite Keoua Kuahuula to the consecration of the heiau. Against the advice of his advisors, Keoua accepted. He sailed his fleet northward toward Kawaihae along the west coast. He stopped at a place called Luahinewai, about 15 miles south of the heiau, where he washed himself and performed a ceremony that was a sure sign that he was preparing himself for death. He then ordered all weapons taken off his double canoe, and called his most trusted chiefs aboard.

It was obvious to all that Keoua Kuahuula had accepted the fact that Kamehameha was the one chosen by the gods — the star with the tail had announced his birth, he had moved the Naha Stone, he was entrusted with the family war god, he had defeated Kiwalao, and the combined fleets of Oahu, Maui, and Molokai had failed to stop the construction of Puukohola Heiau. He himself had been unable to stop it, and even Pele, the volcano goddess, had shown her displeasure by destroying a portion of his army. All was in Kamehameha's favor.

As Keoua Kuahuula's fleet approached the beach in the shadow of the great heiau, even he must have been impressed. Then, he heard Kamehameha calling to him from among the warriors assembled on shore. As Keoua was about to jump off his canoe into the water, one of Kamehameha's chiefs hurled a spear. Keoua caught it and tossed it aside. Then, gunfire was heard, and Keoua and 11 of his men were killed. Their bodies were taken to the heiau and offered as sacrifices to the war god, Kukailimoku. In this way, the heiau was consecrated.

A Unified Hawaii

Kamehameha was very pleased. He now controlled the entire island of Hawaii and could turn his attention toward fulfilling his destiny — all the islands of Hawaii under his rule.

He amassed a great armada of war canoes. They extended for miles on both sides of Upolu Point, all pointing north toward the island of Maui.

First, Maui was taken; then in 1794, the island of Molokai. A year later, Kamehameha advanced his mighty fleet toward Oahu. When his canoes landed, they covered the beaches of Waikiki for many miles.

Herb Kane's painting of the arrival of Keoua Kuahuula at Puukohola Heiau.

The 8,000-man army of Oahu fell back and waited for Kamehameha to advance. They were no match for Kamehameha's 17,000-man strong army. The battle was fierce and the Oahu army was forced into Nuuanu Valley. Surrounded, Oahu's army fought valiantly until they were pushed off the steep cliff, Nuuanu Pali. The chief of Oahu escaped, but was later captured and killed. By the end of 1795, only the island of Kauai eluded Kamehameha.

An invasion of Kauai the following year proved unsuccessful; Kamehameha's fleet was devastated by a storm at sea. Those warriors reaching Kauai were quickly disposed of by the army of Kauai. The surviving canoes limped back to Oahu.

After 15 years of living under the threat of invasion, the king of Kauai agreed to place himself under Kamehameha's rule. In 1810, he sent his son to Kamehameha's court as a hostage to ensure his loyalty.

With his dream finally realized, a weary Kamehameha returned to the warm, sunny coast of Kona on the island of Hawaii in 1812. He administered the affairs of the kingdom from his residence at Kamakahonu (the eye of the turtle), on the grounds of the present-day Hotel King Kamehameha in Kailua-Kona. He remained there until his death on May 8, 1819.

Puukohola Heiau National Historic Site at Kawaihae was authorized by Congress on August 17, 1972. On the hillside between Puukohola Heiau and the sea are the ruins of **Mailekini Heiau,** a temple used by Kamehameha's ancestors. This temple was said to be nearly equal to Puukohola Heiau in dimensions. It appeared to have been literally crowded with images, but no human sacrifices were offered to any of its gods. During Kamehameha's time, this temple was converted by John Young into a fort to protect Kawaihae.

A third temple, **Hale o Kapuni Heiau,** is believed to be submerged just offshore of Puukohola. Future archeological work is planned to determine the location and extent of the ruins of the temple, which was dedicated to the shark gods.

Other points of interest close to the Heiaus are **Pelekane,** the site of the king's residence at Kawaihae. King Kamehameha II returned here after the death of his father in 1819 to prepare for his role as king of the Hawaiian Islands. The site of **John Young's house** can also be found here.

A statue of Kamehameha I stands at Kapaau in North Kohala.

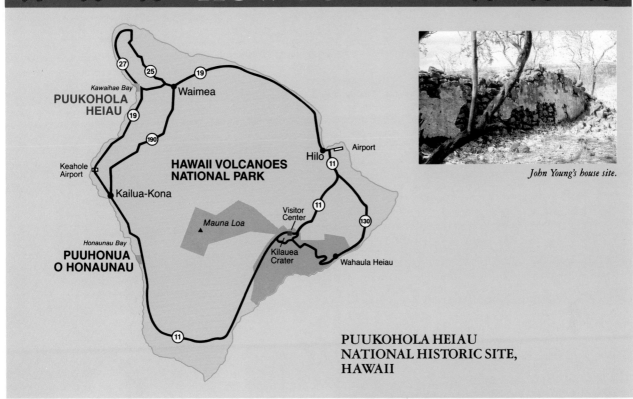

John Young's house site.

PUUKOHOLA HEIAU NATIONAL HISTORIC SITE, HAWAII

Location

Puukohola Heiau National Historic Site is located one mile away from Kawaihae on the northwest coast of Hawaii and about 12 miles west of Waimea-Kohala.

How To Get There

Airlines make scheduled flights several times daily from Honolulu to airports at Hilo and Keahole. Taxis and cars may be rented at all airports.

Information

The **Visitor Center** is open from 7:30 a.m. until 4 p.m. daily. However, the **Puukohola Heiau, the Mailekini Heiau** and the **John Young House** site can be viewed from outside 24 hours a day. They are not open to the public due to religious, preservation and safety reasons. The waterworn stones used in the construction slip easily and there is great potential that anyone climbing on them may be hurt.

A self-guiding trail and interpretive folder take the visitor around the major sites in the park. Orientation talks are given daily at the Visitor Center. Guided tours can be arranged if advance notification is given.

Special Events

Special programs on Hawaiian history and culture are presented several times a year, and Hawaiian and environmental study workshops can be arranged for groups in advance.

The park holds an annual two-day cultural festival on the weekend closest to August 17, the anniversary of the park's authorization. Royal processions, craft workshops, Hawaiian games and food tasting take place.

The Waimea Hawaiian Civic Club also presents a weekly craft workshop from January through September. This is funded by the Hawaii Natural History Association, which also helps fund part of the cultural festival.

An aerial view of Puukohola Heiau.

Tips

The park site is a fragile, desert environment. Please be sure to stay on the designated trails. Those hiking the trail are encouraged to prepare themselves with cool clothing, sunscreen, and suitable footwear, as the trail is long and hot. Climbing on the walls of the temple is prohibited for safety reasons. You are also requested not to smoke as the area is very dry and windy and grass fires easily start. Bathing in front of the Heiau is not permitted due to the silted nature of the water at this point. Swimming and picnicking are both available at nearby Spencer Beach Park. Gas and grocery supplies may be purchased at Kawaihae.

MOLOKAI

The North Molokai coast from
Kalawao Park, Kalaupapa Peninsula.

Kalaupapa
National Historical Park

Kalaupapa presents some of the most beautiful and spectacular scenery in all Hawaii. The same steep cliffs and rugged seas that made it a perfect spot for isolation in the past now combine with its history to create a site worthy of designation as a National Historical Park. The park has significant natural and archeological resources but its history and its residents are the primary resource. The establishment of Kalaupapa National Historical Park in 1980 was an official recognition of the importance of Hawaii's experience with leprosy, also called Hansen's Disease, to the nation and the world.

The principal purposes of the park are to preserve and interpret its history while providing a well-maintained community in which the Kalaupapa residents are guaranteed they may live out their lives with the assurance that their lifestyle and privacy will be protected. Important historical structures, traditional Hawaiian sites, cultural values, and natural features are to be maintained and limited visitation by the public allowed.

There are currently just under 100 patients residing at the Settlement, most of whom are between the ages of 50 and 80. The advent of sulfone drugs as a cure for Hansen's Disease in the 1940s eliminated the need for isolation and all new cases are treated strictly on an outpatient basis.

Although free to leave the Settlement, most of the residents of Kalaupapa have spent a major part of their lives there, regard it as home, and have chosen to remain. They are free to come and go as they please but the stigma that is still associated with the disease prevents many from feeling comfortable in the community at large. Nevertheless, several have traveled around the world and trips to Las Vegas are commonplace. This was not the case, however, throughout most of Kalaupapa's history. The current residents of the Settlement provide a valuable link with the past. Their recollections provide a firm foundation upon which the story of Kalaupapa, and the history of leprosy in Hawaii, can be interpreted for the education and inspiration of future generations.

A Special History

Hawaii provides a unique opportunity to interpret the effects of a leprosy epidemic on individuals and society for it is possible to trace the course of an

The Kalaupapa Landing (probably in the 1920s).

epidemic over a period of about 150 years in a geographically small but culturally diverse area. Hawaii's contributions to the treatment of this disease, both medically and socially, are great, and the history of leprosy in Hawaii presents a powerful means with which to educate the public about the realities of a disease that has been shrouded for centuries in myths, misconceptions, fear, and ignorance.

The origin of leprosy in Hawaii can be traced back to several well-authenticated cases noted among the Hawaiians in the 1830s. Reports of the disease became more common in the 1850s, and by the 1860s, expressions of concern and alarm echoed throughout the kingdom. The disease became an official concern on January 3, 1865, when an "Act to Prevent the Spread of Leprosy" was signed into law by King Kamehameha V. This act authorized the setting apart of land for the purpose of isolating any person with leprosy who might spread the disease if left "at large." On January 6, 1866, the first "shipment" of patients was made to the leprosy settlement on the Kalawao side of the Makanalua peninsula, north shore of Molokai.*

Conditions at the Settlement were a constant source of controversy. Food and shelter were inadequate and for many years, no doctor could be found to reside there. The patients felt they were being sent to Kalawao to die and consequently saw no reason to abide by

---

*The Makanalua peninsula is only a small part of Molokai and is divided into three sections, Kalawao, Makanalua, and Kalaupapa, the distance between Kalaupapa and Kalawao being about two and a half miles.

any rules. For many years, the Settlement existed in a state of lawlessness where the strong dominated the weak and those whose leprosy was very advanced were at the mercy of those in whom the disease was still in its early stages.

Father Damien

In time, conditions at the Settlement improved somewhat and two churches and a hospital were built. However, law and order could not be maintained, for crimes were committed with no fear of punishment. Indeed, what punishment could be worse than that which fate had already dealt them? These were the conditions faced by a Belgian priest, Father Damien, when he arrived at the Settlement in 1873. He was the first priest to remain at Kalawao and live with the people, and the first white man in whom they put their trust. Damien showed no fear of the patients or their disease and treated them as friends rather than outcasts. In addition, he gave them something that no one before him had been able to give, the hope that things would get better—if not in this life, then in the next.

Father Damien was

St. Philomena: Father Damien's Church, Kalawao.

Kalaupapa Lighthouse.

Dramatic Kalaupapa surf pounds the rugged coast.

officially diagnosed as having leprosy in 1885 and died four years later. His inspiring life and death among his people at the Settlement alerted the world to the prob-

Father Damien in 1889.

lem of leprosy and the plight of its victims. Many expected interest in the Settlement to subside after Damien's death, but this did not happen. Brother Joseph Dutton, who went to Molokai in 1886 to assist Damien, worked among the patients for 44 years. During this time he was instrumental in keeping the world informed on life at the Settlement. Scattered in archives and personal collections around the United States, Dutton's letters provide valuable insights into the early years of the Settlement's existence.

Mother Marianne came to Hawaii in 1883 and to Molokai in 1888. She nursed those suffering from leprosy for 35 years, yet her name is not well known. The magnitude and importance of her contribution to the care and treatment of this disease in Hawaii is largely unrecognized due to her strong desire for anonymity. An oustanding administrator, nurse and pharmacist, Mother Marianne felt it was essential to preserve the dignity of the patients and instill in them a "quality-of-life" spirit. No matter how hopeless a situation was or how close to death the person was, he knew he was not forgotten and was allowed and encouraged to live and die with dignity.

Robert Louis Stevenson was extremely impressed when he visited the Settlement in 1889 and commented, "As for the girls in the Bishop Home, of the many beautiful things I have been privileged to see in this life, they, and what has been done for them, is not the least beautiful." Inspired by his visit, he later wrote, ". . . I never admired my poor race so much, nor (strange as it may seem) loved life more than in the Settlement."

The Bishop Home for Girls, Kalaupapa, in 1904.

John Cambra, aged 82, at the site of the Baldwin Home for Boys, his first home upon arrival at the Settlement in 1924.

Kalawao today.

A Model Community

In the early 1900s, improvements at the Settlement, resulting largely from the efforts of Dr. W.J. Goodhue, Resident Physician, and J.D. McVeigh, Superintendent, with the continued guidance of Mother Marianne, again focused attention on Kalaupapa as a model center for the treatment of leprosy. Most of the patients had moved from Kalawao to Kalaupapa in the 1890s and a major building program was undertaken at Kalaupapa in 1907. That year and again in 1915, Jack London traveled to the Settlement and was inspired to write extensively about what he saw. He concluded that the chief horror of leprosy was in the minds of those who had never seen a patient and did not know anything about the disease.

Conditions continued to improve. By the 1920s, and especially after the advent of sulfone drugs as a cure for the disease in the 1940s, patients began to live longer and healthier lives. The quality of life was enhanced by increased participation in sports, fishing, choral groups, and clubs.

Triumph Over the Odds

As was the case with many notable visitors in the past, including Robert Louis Stevenson, modern-day tourists are often attracted to the Settlement because of their interest in Father Damien. With little knowledge of the present-day realities of leprosy or Hansen's Disease, many visitors still think of the Settlement and the disease in terms of Father Damien's time and arrive expecting to be depressed. Almost without exception, they leave inspired.

The early history of Kalaupapa and those who devoted their lives to the Settlement serves to attract and move visitors, but it is the patients themselves who have always inspired those with whom they come into contact, from Father Damien and Stevenson to present-day administrators and writers. It is their story that makes Kalaupapa National Historical Park unique. The park stands as a monument to their ability to endure and overcome, both physically and spiritually, not only disease, but man's inhumanity to man.

Facts About Hansen's Disease

Hansen's Disease is a chronic, infectious disease caused by a germ, *Mycobacterium leprae,* which usually involves the nerves, skin and eyes. There are approximately 11 million cases of Hansen's Disease in the world, about 5,000 of which are in the United States. Hansen's Disease is transmitted by direct, person-to-person contact, usually repetitive, over a prolonged period of time. However, it is one of the least contagious of all communicable diseases and only about 4-5% of the world's population is even susceptible to it. Since the mid-40s, sulfone antibiotics have been used in the treatment of Hansen's Disease and now two or three antibiotics are used simultaneously to shorten treatment time. With this regimen, the infection is cured and within a few days or weeks of care, even the most contagious patient becomes noninfectious. Isolation is a thing of the past and all new cases are treated strictly on an outpatient basis. Although Hansen's Disease is the official term in Hawaii, and also advocated by others in the United States, the term "leprosy" is used throughout most of the world. The question of terminology is widely debated; however, it is universally agreed that the term "leper" should never be used. Use of this word takes away a person's individuality and unfairly characterizes him solely on the basis of his disease.

HOW TO VISIT

KALAUPAPA
NATIONAL HISTORICAL
PARK

Bayview Home, Kalaupapa.

KALAUPAPA
NATIONAL HISTORICAL PARK,
MOLOKAI

Location

Kalaupapa National Historical Park is located on the central northern peninsula of the island of Molokai. The area is relatively inaccessible and can only be entered by air, mule or foot.

How To Get There

In order to protect the privacy and lifestyle of the residents, all visitors to Kalaupapa National Historical Park must be at least 16 years old and either be part of a guided tour, be an invited guest, or have special permission from the Department of Health. Visitation is limited to 100 visitors a day. Two small airports serve the island—one at Hoolehua, the other flying directly into the Kalaupapa Settlement.

Visitors arriving at Hoolehua Airport can obtain a magnificent view of Kalaupapa from the 2,000-foot cliff overlooking the Settlement. It is approximately a six-mile drive to the vista point. To reach the Settlement by mule, you will need to make arrangements on Molokai with a company running tours as far as Kalaupapa. Several airlines fly small planes directly into Kalaupapa Airport. Once in the Islands, inquire at your local travel desk to make flight arrangements. Hikers and those flying in must contact one of the two tour companies at Kalaupapa owned by residents.

These two tour companies conduct the daily tours of the Settlement. A small fee is charged. For more information, contact Damien Tours or Ike's Scenic Tours, Kalaupapa, Molokai, Hawaii 96742. It is also possible to make brief visits to Kalaupapa via helicopter or light airplane. These tours are done early morning and evening and do not coincide with the main tours of the Settlement.

The Kalaupapa Peninsula.

Information

The four-hour tour of Kalaupapa takes the visitor around the community, stopping at key points of interest such as Father Damien's church, other churches in the area and Mother Marianne's grave. Visitors should bring a packed lunch since no meals are available.

Tips

Visitors are reminded that the Kalaupapa Settlement exists to provide an opportunity for the residents to live a quiet, private existence. Appropriate behavior is requested at all times. Be prepared to spend an entire day traveling to and from the community—there are occasional delays in transportation.

The USS Arizona Memorial

F ew people living in 1941 can forget where they were on December 7. The day was burned indelibly in memory when they learned of the Pearl Harbor attack. All who heard the news knew that the world would never again be the same.

Today at Pearl Harbor, the USS *Arizona* Memorial evokes these memories for millions of visitors, even those born after 1941. The National Park Service has operated the visitor program at the memorial and its shoreside center since 1980. From the memorial, visitors can view the battleship *Arizona,* which sank with more than a thousand of her crew, a silent but moving reminder of the tragedy.

Questions linger over the events of that day. How did it happen? Why were U.S. forces caught by surprise? As relations between Japan and the United States grew worse in 1940 and 1941, Japan's leaders became convinced that war was inevitable. They decided to begin the conflict by striking first.

The Pearl Harbor attack force, centered around six aircraft carriers and their 400-plus planes, was commanded by Vice Admiral Chuichi Nagumo. Undetected, Nagumo's carriers approached Pearl Harbor from the north and launched a strike force of 353 planes shortly after dawn on Sunday, December 7, 1941.

As Japanese airmen winged toward their target, an American radar set on the north shore of Oahu picked up the planes. The two privates manning the station reported the contact, but their concern was dismissed. Nothing more than a group of American planes expected that morning from California, explained the officer in charge of the control center.

Braced for swarms of American fighter planes and a barrage of anti-aircraft fire, the raiders were stunned to find only empty skies and ships sitting peacefully at anchor. First to find their targets were the torpedo planes. In the opening moments of the attack they struck the *Nevada, Arizona, Oklahoma, West Virginia, California, Utah, Raleigh,* and *Helena.* Those on deck for church services or waiting for liberty launches stared uncomprehendingly. Was this another drill?

A rainbow frames the USS Arizona *Memorial.*

I didn't really know we were under attack. It just didn't dawn on me that we were actually in a war. I felt the impact as the torpedo hit the forward part of the ship. Next thing I knew, they were sounding general quarters. Dummies that we were, we went down to the battle stations, and found that all the watertight doors were open and we were up to our waists in water and trying to close the doors. The next thing we knew, it was Abandon Ship! Abandon Ship!
—Clark J. Simmons, USS *Utah*

Other Japanese planes struck nearby air bases simultaneously. So complete was the surprise that few American fighters rose to challenge Japanese control of the skies. Mechanics and ground crewmen were cut down as they tried desperately to move the planes out of danger and prepare them for takeoff.

I was running for Hangar 11, and the hangar got a direct hit right in front of me. I couldn't get up and walk because of the way my leg was broken. While I was crawling there, one of these strafers got me with a bullet just below the right knee and down the side of my left leg. I'm just so damn mad because I'm so helpless. I remembered this .45 in my hip pocket, [but] my wrist was broken and I didn't even know it. My hand was just useless, so I couldn't get the gun going. It made me so damn mad I just took the thing and threw it. —Harold Lenburg, Hickam Field

The torpedo planes were followed by high-level horizontal bombers which rained armor-piercing bombs on the dying ships. Hardest hit was the *Arizona*. One bomb struck the battleship's forward ammunition magazine. The bow erupted and the ship sank within minutes, carrying 1,177 of her crew to the bottom.

After the *Arizona* exploded I put a group in the boat—10 or 12 sailors. We got to the *Arizona* and we just stepped over the railing onto the deck, but it was hot, very hot. The whole bow all the way back for 200 feet looked like a giant plow had plowed the steel up...great jagged pieces and fire coming out everywhere. I told the men, "Check any open hatches." They scrambled in all directions and came back and said that every hatch had fire coming out of it, and there couldn't be anyone living here because they'd had one terrible explosion. So I says, 'Well, get back in the boat. There's nothing we can do here.'
—L.B. Luckenbach, USS *California*

In less than two hours, American military might in the Pacific had been crippled. Twenty-one vessels—eight battleships, three cruisers, four destroyers, and six auxiliaries—had been sunk or damaged. Nearly 200 planes had been reduced to wreckage. And 2,403 Americans were dead. Japanese losses were light by comparison: 29 planes and 55 aircrewmen, less than 10 percent of the attack force, failed to return to their carriers. In addition, one Japanese fleet submarine, five midget submarines (which failed to inflict any damage), and their crews were lost.

Despite its undeniable success, the blow was not

The USS Arizona *burns after her forward magazines explode following the Japanese attack on Pearl Harbor on December 7, 1941.*

Construction of the USS Arizona *Memorial, completed in 1962.*

The dedication of the Memorial on May 30, 1962.

enough to ensure Japanese victory. Most of the ships sunk at Pearl Harbor were raised and lived to fight another day. Only the *Arizona, Utah,* and *Oklahoma* were unsalvageable. The Japanese failed to damage any U.S. aircraft carriers (by a stroke of luck they were all absent from the harbor on December 7). The attackers also neglected to hit the naval repair and supply facilities at Pearl Harbor. Most importantly, the Japanese miscalculated the American reaction. Instead of discouragement and dejection, the surprise attack roused the nation to a furious resolve to exact revenge.

Building the Arizona Memorial

For years after the end of World War II, the twisted wreckage of the *Arizona* lay neglected in the shallows of Pearl Harbor. As time passed, however, many began to recognize the need to commemorate the events of December 7, 1941. The territory of Hawaii established the Pacific War Memorial Commission to select sites and raise funds for war memorials in Hawaii. The commission selected the *Arizona's* remains as the most fitting site for a memorial and began to collect contributions.

In 1958, the commission sponsored a benefit concert by Elvis Presley and a special broadcast of the television show "This Is Your Life." Both events raised money for construction of the *Arizona* Memorial. To supplement the private donations raised by the Pacific War Memorial Commission, the state of Hawaii and the federal government appropriated funds for the memorial.

Honolulu architect Alfred Preis designed the memorial as a cantilevered span bridging the hulk of the *Arizona.* The most striking elements of the design are the curved roofline which dips in the center and rises to a peak at each end, and the 21 large openings in the sides and roof of the structure. Over the years these features have acquired symbolic significance. The 21 openings are commonly interpreted as symbolizing a perpetual 21-gun salute for the *Arizona's* dead; the dip in the roofline is taken to represent the initial defeat, with the peaks signifying the ultimate American victory in World War II.

Completed in 1962 at a cost of $500,000, the *Arizona* Memorial was an instant success. Visitors waited for Navy shuttle boats in ever-longer lines at a nondescript dockside, frequently exposed to inclement weather. As the lines got longer, the need for a shoreside visitor center became more obvious.

In 1975, the *Arizona* Memorial Museum Foundation began a drive to raise funds for a shore facility. The center would house movie theaters, a museum, and administrative offices. The foundation raised nearly $1,000,000. With an additional $4,000,000 in federal

The large wall at the far end of the Memorial commemorates all those aboard the USS Arizona *who lost their lives during the attack on Pearl Harbor.*

funds, the shoreside visitor center was completed in 1980. At that point, the Navy handed over administration of the memorial and the shoreside center to the National Park Service.

USS Arizona Underwater Dive Survey

In 1983-84, the *Arizona* Memorial Museum Association funded an underwater survey in which U.S. Navy and Park Service divers inspected the remains of the USS *Arizona*. From the beginning of the project, the Park Service decided that no divers would enter the interior of the vessel. There were two reasons for that decision: first, respect for the dead entombed within the *Arizona;* second, the danger of divers becoming trapped inside the twisted wreckage.

Once the divers began their explorations, they made a number of important discoveries. Most reassuring was that the *Arizona's* remains appeared to be stable and posed no danger to visitors or the memorial structure. The divers examined the areas of the ship devastated by the explosion which sank the *Arizona*. They found the forward section almost entirely demolished and the upper decks in that area collapsed a full 20 feet by the blast. Amazingly, though, the ship's Number 1 gun turret, its giant 14-inch guns intact, was found in its original position atop the demolished deck.

For years, visitors had been puzzled by a film of oil which appears on the water near the *Arizona*. Divers discovered that the oil, leaking from the ship's fuel tanks, rises from the area near the Number 3 gun turret at a rate of four drops per minute. No one knows how much oil is left in the tanks, so the leak may continue for decades to come.

The divers found many haunting mementos of the *Arizona's* life and death: firehoses abandoned by the

The Memorial is extremely popular with visitors to Pearl Harbor.

crew when the flames overwhelmed their efforts to control her fires; a porthole with an air bubble trapped between two panes of glass; open hatchways used by the crew as they abandoned the doomed ship. These and other features were recorded on film and left undisturbed. Today, and for the future, the *Arizona* rests in peace, standing as silent but eloquent testimony to the tragedy of that long-ago Sunday morning.

A perspective view from the stern of the USS Arizona. *Inset: Divers measure base lines which will be used to study changes in the* Arizona's *condition.*

HOW TO VISIT

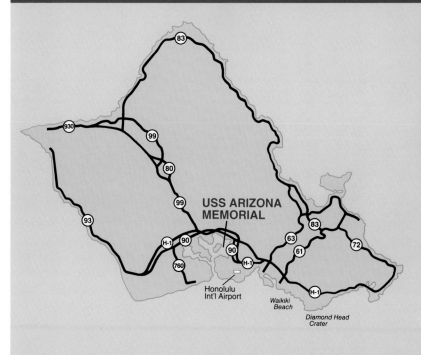

Visitors are taken by launch from the Visitor Center to the Memorial.

USS ARIZONA MEMORIAL, OAHU

Location

The USS *Arizona* Memorial is located in Pearl Harbor on the island of Oahu, close to the Honolulu International Airport.

How To Get There

It's easy to get to the USS *Arizona* Memorial. If you're traveling by car from Waikiki, go west on the H-1 Freeway, and take the airport cutoff; the *Arizona* Memorial exit is about a mile past the Honolulu International Airport. If you're using the city bus, take the Pearl Harbor bus from the Waikiki/Ala Moana area. There is also a private bus company which runs a shuttle between the major hotels and the memorial.

Information

The visitor program operates seven days a week from 8:00 a.m. to 3:00 p.m. To visit the *Arizona* Memorial, go to the information desk in the Visitor Center lobby and pick up a ticket for your tour. Tickets are issued on a first-come, first-served basis. Your ticket will have a tour number printed on the front.

When your tour number is announced, you'll go to the theater. After watching a short film about the Pearl Harbor attack, you will board a shuttle boat that will take you to the *Arizona* Memorial. There you may disembark and go aboard the memorial.

From the memorial, you can see the deck of the *Arizona* lying just beneath the surface of the water. Oil seeping from the ship's fuel tanks forms a rainbow-like film on the water's surface. The *Arizona* Memorial's flagstaff is mounted on the base of the battleship's main mast, which was cut off just above the waterline. Also above the waterline is the base of the *Arizona's* Number 3 gun turret. The names of the *Arizona's* 1,177 dead are inscribed on the wall of the shrine

The entrance to the Memorial.

room at the far end of the memorial.

After you've had a chance to visit the memorial, you can go back to the Visitor Center on any returning shuttle boat. The time required for the film and the round trip to the *Arizona* Memorial is about 60-90 minutes. An open plan museum located in the Visitor Center exhibits photographs and memorabilia illustrating the events of December 7. Next door, a wide range of gifts are available from the bookstore. Snacks may be purchased in the center.

Rules and Tips

The rules for *Arizona* Memorial are simple and few: children are welcome to view the film, but because of safety regulations, they must be at least 45″ tall to board the shuttle boats; no eating, drinking or smoking is permitted in the theaters, aboard the boats, or on the memorial.

The weather at the memorial is liable to be warm but windy, with a change of rain. Cool clothing is recommended with a light, waterproof coverup.

War In The Pacific National Historical Park

Gaan Point, Guam.

Established in 1978, War in the Pacific National Historical Park is the only area managed by the National Park Service in the Territory. The park was created by Congress to commemorate the bravery and sacrifice of those participating in the campaigns of the Pacific Theater of World War II, and to conserve and interpret outstanding natural, scenic, and historical values and objects on the island of Guam.

History

Guam was originally "discovered" by the western world in 1521 by the Ferdinand Magellan expedition and claimed by Spain 40 years later. Spanish missionaries arrived in 1668, and the native Chamorro religion was displaced by Spanish-Catholic Christianity. The conflicts between the Spanish and Chamorro cultures led to a reduction in native population from an estimated 50,000 to 5,000. When acquired by the United States after the Spanish-American War in 1898, Guam was placed under the Department of the Navy and designated as a Naval Station.

All elements of Guamanian life—predominantly a rural farming culture, centering around family and church—were governed by a paternalistic martial law. Various attempts were made in the U.S. Congress to allow self-government on Guam. However, Navy Department pressure retained the island as a military base. Being a minor naval station, Guam merely served as a refueling stop of American ships heading from Hawaii to the Philippines. International agreements and Congressional fear that fortifying Guam would provoke war with Japan caused all defenses to be removed in 1931.

In 1941, Japan launched a successful campaign to gain control of Asiatic lands under western colonial masters. Guam was particularly attractive because of its strategic location as a launch site for twin-engine bombers and Zeros. The Japanese also wanted to thwart any attempt by the United States to use Guam as a way-point en route to the Philippines. The takeover began on December 10, 1941, and ended before dawn the next day. During the next 30 months of Japanese occupation, Japanese language schools were installed and English banned. Chamorros were forced into serving the Japanese. They built hundreds of defensive installations and several airstrips, and dug numerous shelter caves to house Japanese soldiers.

Guam and Saipan began to play a strategic role in 1944, as the American forces island-hopped in an effort to defeat the Japanese. Airbases within flying range of Japan were essential to reducing the Japanese empire. When the Americans arrived to recapture the island in 1944, they met a Japanese force of about 18,500. Of that number, only 1,250 were taken prisoner—the rest died in the conflict or committed suicide. American losses consisted of 2,124 killed and some 5,250 wounded. The number of Guamanians lost is unknown (most of the Chamorros were in concentration camps away from the battles).

The Park

Guam's six park units are scattered along the western edge of the island at sites significant to the American recapture of Guam in July 1944. The northern invasion beach is encompassed by the **Asan Beach Unit,** where the present **Visitor Center** is located. Looking out over the Philippine Sea, visitors are encouraged to envision how the horizon, packed with American war ships, must have appeared then to the entrenched Japanese.

Further inland, where fierce fighting took place, the **Asan Inland Unit** still shows scars from American bombing. Numerous caves and war relics litter the jungle floor. Some munitions still surface and visitors are advised to watch out for these hazardous reminders of past conflicts. The Inland Unit is undeveloped and while not closed to entry, the jungle is a formidable obstacle to easy hiking. Future plans for this area include hiking trails and nature study areas, in addition to war-related interpretation.

At the top of the ridge overlooking Agana, the **Fonte Plateau** provides a spectacular view of the countryside below. It was used as the command post of General Takashina, who commanded the Japanese occupation forces. Several cave systems penetrate the cliffs and were strongholds for their Japanese residents. The Unit was added to the park in 1984 and remains undeveloped.

The southern invasion beach is included in the **Agat Unit.** Situated adjacent to the village of Agat, the developed areas of **Gaan Point, Apaca Point,** and **Rizal Beach** afford the opportunity to view some of the remaining Japanese defenses. Heavy bombing has left many of these sites in various stages of disrepair. Time and the tropical climate have also taken their toll on the concrete and reinforced-steel structures hastily constructed by forced Chamorro labor.

As elements of the First Provisional Marine Brigade pushed ashore at Agat and captured the Orote Peninsula, they faced resistance from the Japanese forces entrenched along the slopes of Mount Alifan. This park unit overlooks the village of Agat from the east and provides a panoramic view of the entire southern invasion area. The **Alifan Unit** is presently inaccessible to the public due to the private and military lands that surround it, but future plans call for interpretative sites and trails.

During the invasion, the American forces constantly searched for the rumored shore guns that were believed to overlook Apra Harbor. The guns were there, near Piti village, but not yet operational. Today, they stand as stark reminders of the strength of the Japanese fortifications. The **Piti Guns Unit** located on the hillside overlooking the village of Piti gives visitors a firsthand look at three of the five-inch shore guns. The unit also provides an opportunity to see the remnants of a mahogany forest. The area is reached by a trail from the church in Piti, but visitors are reminded that access to this area of the park is through private lands and landowners' rights must be respected.

The final park unit is the **Mt. Tenjo/Mt. Chachao** area. It was at these 1,000-foot mountain summits that American forces from both the northern and southern assaults joined to form a perimeter around the beachhead and Apra Harbor.

As well as interpreting World War II, the park is also concerned with protecting and interpreting the natural and cultural resources. Toward this goal, the park units include beautiful jungles of lush vegetation and offshore coral reefs. Chamorro cultural programs are in development and will be presented in several of the units. As with all newly established areas, the park has a wide range of challenges to meet. Its future will depend very much on funding, land acquisition, and the development of exhibits, nature and historical trails, and marine and beach recreational sites. Remote Guam's part in World War II was small but vital. Her story is preserved here in War in the Pacific National Historical Park.

HOW TO VISIT

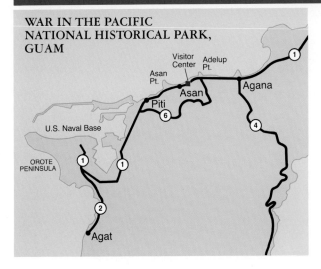

WAR IN THE PACIFIC NATIONAL HISTORICAL PARK, GUAM

Adelup Point, the ocean side of the road is within the boundary until you reach Asan Point. The Visitor Center is located at Asan. The Agat Unit lies south of Naval Station Guam and with the exception of the developed areas of Gaan, Apaca and Rizal, is primarily offshore waters. The other units are located inland and to reach them you will need directions from the Visitor Center.

Information
The major battle sites are scattered over a fairly large area. Be sure to pick up a self-guiding brochure at the Visitor Center in Asan before starting your drive around the park. The events surrounding the war years (1941-1945) are depicted through photos and a collection of memorabilia in the small museum located at the Visitor Center.

Tips
The weather in Guam is subtropical, averaging 82 degrees Fahrenheit, therefore summer clothing is recommended. Although the wet season runs from August to November, rainfall on the island is quite frequent during other seasons, so be sure to pack raingear. You will be required to clear customs on arrival. United States citizens do not need a passport to visit Guam but visitors from other countries will be required to produce one. Guam has beautiful coral reefs and is one of the richest shelling areas in the Pacific, so bring a swimsuit and snorkeling/diving gear. Some sea creatures are extremely hazardous—please check before you touch!

Location
Guam is located about 3300 miles west of Hawaii. The island is 212 square miles in size with a pleasant tropical climate.

How To Get There
Air travel to the island is primarily from Japan and secondarily from Hawaii, with numerous flights daily. To reach War in the Pacific National Historical Park, drive south on Marine Drive from the airport near Agana. Once you reach

CHART OF SERVICES AVAILABLE IN THE PACIFIC PARKS

PARK	VISITOR CENTER	EXHIBIT	MUSEUM	HANDICAPPED ACCESS/RR	NPS GUIDED TOUR	SELF-GUIDED TOUR	PICNIC AREA	CAMPGROUND	BACKCOUNTRY USE PERMIT	HIKING	FISHING	CABIN RENTAL	HOTEL	RESTAURANT/ SNACKS	ENVIRON-MENTAL STDY	LIVING HIST. PROGRAM	GROUP CAMPSITE	SWIMMING (unsupervised)	HORSEBACK RIDING	MEDICAL
HAWAII VOLCANOES NATIONAL PARK Hawaii National Park, HI 96718	■	■	■	■	■	■	■	■	■	■	■	■	■	■		■	■			
HALEAKALA NATIONAL PARK P.O. Box 537, Makawao, Maui, HI 96768	■	■	■	■	■	■	■	■	■	■	■					■			■	■
PUUHONUA O HONAUNAU NATIONAL HISTORICAL PARK, P.O. Box 128, Honaunau, Kona, HI 96726	■	■	■	■		■	■			■	■					■		■		
PUUKOHOLA HEIAU NATIONAL HISTORIC SITE P.O. Box 4963, Kawaihae, HI 96743	■	■	■	■		■				■						■				
KALAUPAPA NATIONAL HISTORICAL PARK Kalaupapa, Molokai, HI 96742 *Private guided tour only		■				*	■													■
USS ARIZONA MEMORIAL 1 Arizona Memorial Place, Honolulu, HI 96818	■	■	■	■	■	■									■					
WAR IN THE PACIFIC NATIONAL HISTORICAL PARK Marine Drive, Asan, P.O. Box FA, Agana, Guam 96910	■	■	■	■		■	■			■	■			■						■